𝒬etter
to the
Stranger
Within

An Octogenarian Reflects

Maure Quilter

Gratefully

Maure Quilter

Spring 2017

Azalea Art Press
Berkeley . California

Author Photo:
Vivek Dhar

Cover Painting "Golden Reflections"
and Interior Illustrations:
Barbara Bonds McDaniel

ISBN: 978-1-943471-20-1

A Blessing

Before my beloved readers dip into my "first born" book,
I pray that this book may encourage, bless, heal, inspire
and transform whoever desires
these attributes in their lives.

Whatever leads readers to this place of
courage, curiosity, hunger or thirst—may they
eventually bear the unique distinct fruit needed
in each life journey.

Whoever visits my journey, no matter the spirituality,
religious origin or simply a craving to be one with truth
and goodness and integrity, be blessed.
May this first attempt feed, nourish, and satisfy you.

This lifetime (now) is all we have here on earth.
So search it out, dig deeply. Experience nature, art, music,
film, dance, precious animals and others.

Prod, stir, stop, look, listen. Listen to one's own gentle
inner whispers. Take careful note.

Embrace courage. Find soul mates of your same stripe.
Find soul mates contrary to you. Make room (lots) for
differences. Exclude none. Learn and grow from even
those to whom you feel invisible, even those who
disrespect you and your loved ones.

Embrace the homeless, the mentally distressed,
all those human beings who speak, act, live differently.
At least try.

However, if you feel thrown away by anyone no matter
the power, the authority or degree, then "shake the dust
from your sandals and walk to the next village" to share
your gifts, as Jesus said, over and over in His gospels.

Welcome your own inspiration, hero and heroines.
Welcome them all—transcendent beings, deities
known and unknown—all that heal.

"All will be well, every manner of thing will be well,"
Julian of Norwich said so. And so do I.
Take, read, enjoy, and share as you wish.

Written with Deepest Love and Gratefulness,

Maure Quilter
2017

Dedication

I offer this book
to the UnMothered, especially my own Mother,
Mary Ann (Murray) Quilter, born in 1910,
who died of a broken heart (my diagnosis) in 1964.

And to every UnMothered student,
client, stranger, friend . . . all those I've touched
through these many years
of my long Sacred Journey.

I also dedicate this writing to
the Spirit of God within me,
who blessed me with the grace
to "be with" those I met, served, and loved
as whole-heartedly as was possible.

As the wise say:

Amen
So be it

Alleluia

Gifted Team

Barbara Bonds McDaniel

Artist and painter of original cover art and book illustrations, designer of homes and living spaces, of her own life in the Spirit, the mother of Eric (RIP in heaven, 1994), and my inspiration in many ways.

Vivek Dhar

Provided, with permission, my author portrait, an artist with an amazing photographer's timing and eye.

Elizabeth Gilbert

Who taught me through her book *Big Magic* that the gift of writing is your very own child to feed, clothe, protect and support, no matter what.

Colleen Hendricks

Not only my amazing caregiver during a challenging and difficult period, but my transcriber par excellence, mind reader, caretaker of this precious first book.

Karen Mireau

Poet, Literary Midwife, my unexpected gift (thank you Mary Tuchscherer!), seer of souls, seer of potential, giver of gifts and nourishment throughout (food, ideas and encouragement).

Madonna Treadway

Who unknowingly challenged me to dig deeper than I ever wanted to into grief, loss and abandonment and ended up writing her own unique story.

Mary Tuchscherer

AWA (Amherst Writer's & Artists) writer/teacher, my personal muse and inspirer-in-chief, founder of VoiceFlame in the U.S. and Malawi, and 21st century goddess warrior.

My Medical Team 2010 to Present

Insightful Kaiser doctors who singly and together kept me perking along since 2010:
Sara Marie Rotner, MD; Minh T. Huynh, MD; Simon Ashiku, MD; Hugh McElroy, MD; Sam Yang, MD; and Piyush Srivastava, MD.

Prologue

Yes, the book I'm writing is *A Letter to the Stranger Within*. It has evolved into the form of a poem to several Strangers—Strangers who are all me. They are new psyches, having been shocked out of my earlier younger bodies and beginner souls. In each case the Strangers are the new me, stunning my former, more familiar Self.

The First Stranger

The first new Stranger was Maure, eldest of four, in WWII, responsible for my little brother, George Patrick Quilter. We (Mother and I) protected, watched over, and guarded his every move. Patrick (Patsir, his nickname) was brain injured, strong, blonde and blue-eyed. He really was my first child, born when I was three, with my sister Kathy (the wild one) in between us. Age-wise, Kathy was one and Patrick the only infant son. Later, he had terrible tantrums, threw himself downstairs and yet said Mass (pretended to be a Priest). Mother searched for reasons, but we never knew why or how he became brain damaged.

Fast forward to my age nine in 4th grade. Sheila was the fourth child conceived during our Father's only visit home one week to Seattle. Sheila was born nine months later. Our Father still gone to war. Mother was advised by a social worker to send Kathy and me to a movie. It was a sad, sad WWII movie, *Since You Went Away*. We were sent with our babysitter roommate Tara Tolliver. When we came home, Patrick, my precious Patrick, was gone. Not a hint of him remained. No clothes, no toys, no nothing. My Mother was in tears, my Father still "fighting the war."

Patrick disappeared. I never ever saw him again. I went blank. There were no questions, no tears that I recall, no Little Charge to watch, love, care for. He died in an institution at age 26. By then, I was missioned in Tucson, Arizona, a Catholic Sister, and did not attend his funeral and burial in San Diego. Heaven will be my comfort and knowing the Stranger, child Maure, age nine and all I had to confront and learn.

The Second Stranger

As a Catholic nun (teacher and young Principal) in 1972, I gave. I gave until I had no more for myself. I loved people and wanted to help everyone who came into my life. I could not stop or limit my giving. Giving was a part of my soul, my faith, my life. How or what I gave was not important. I simply had no control over my generosity. My personal saying from Scripture was "Silver and gold I have none, what I have I give."

I felt I carried all the world on my shoulders. I went out to all in need. I grew more and more tired. I felt more and more worn out. My inner resources were not helping. My time off was not relaxing. I did not enjoy friends, huge trees, the ocean or the other things I had previously enjoyed. I was becoming over-extended and slowly sinking into a depression of which I knew nothing about. My friends tried to warn me. Even a stranger I met told me he saw I was carrying the world on my shoulders. Somehow I felt obliged to do God's job . . . to take care of His world.

I believed I was committed to do God's worrying. One terrible night my world cracked open. I felt as if I'd died of thirst. There seemed no medical reason for this strong unquenchable thirst. I felt for all the world as if I had crossed over into Heaven. Then after that wonderful other world, I awakened surrounded by the dark. I was helpless. I cried. I babbled. I slept all the day long and then couldn't sleep at night. I called my new psychiatrist and put myself into the hospital. The psych unit was filled with human beings in pain, just like me. Yes, the hospital was dreary. It was painted an awful sickly green. No one had a private room. And there was the terrifying locked unit. Stricken faces peered out of locked glass windows. This scene terrified me. Yet I felt safe there.

At first, I felt raw and even my skin hurt. Eating was not interesting. Television was noisy. Reading (my first love) was impossible. My strong, good, kind doctor who probed ever so gently seemed not to be able to help me. In the hospital, Dr. Colbert insisted on bringing me a cup of coffee for our "visit." As horrible as hospital coffee was, his gift of serving me probably had more to do with my healing than anything he said. Some friends came to visit, but could not help. I felt totally alone. For a short time, I felt even God had forgotten me. God was my mainstay from earliest childhood. Not now.

After several weeks, I began to let the love of the staff help me. Slowly, ever so slowly, I felt something in me knitting together, a new healing. I still would not join in unit activities. I was still lost and in pain. But I did let others care for me for the first time. It was a good feeling to depend on them to care for me as I had cared for others before. Slowly, slowly, this healing came.

Healing felt like waking up on a warm spring morning and smelling fresh-baked bread and bacon and roses blooming just for me. I still had miles and miles to go. I desperately needed therapy with my doctor. I had to examine what must change in my old life. I needed my doctor's support to know that this awful thing would not happen again, ever.

I saw I needed to care for myself first and allow others to help me heal. I needed to tell my own story, all of my story. The doctor kept asking me: "What do you want?" I said: "I want to be well and strong, normal, not a nut case from a psych ward." Slowly, I saw all by myself that I did have to change my whole attitude toward life. I had to take one day at a time, one hour of each day and make it. I had to treat myself as I treated others, gently with love and support.

I could still use my gifts and help others, but I had to be very careful to whom I gave my energy. Even in the hospital I could share my love with others and I did. In most psych units, the patients are assigned tasks. For some reason, I was assigned to be the welcome committee—a committee of one. Actually, this assignment was exactly the wrong job for someone like me, a professional giver! Of course, I liked the assignment. I could welcome and comfort the new arrivals. The enormous problem was the new patients thought and convinced themselves I was a staff member. The irony of this was lost on me at the time.

One day all the patients were off on a "field trip" to Sea World. (I did not want to be in public with a label "psych ward field trip.") Our chaperones were dressed in psych tech white scrubs. Somehow down deep I refused to be grouped in such a way. I seemed to retain a bit of fight. *I would win, be normal,* I told myself.

That day an older grandmother (probably my age now!) and I were left alone to visit in the dreary common room. Grandma, too, refused to go on the trip, but she went further. She refused to speak to her daughter, in fact anyone, for days. We sat that day and I talked. This went on for hours with no response or recognition. Then, somehow she spoke out, "I want to bake cookies in class tomorrow." She had heard me all the time. Then, it was like nothing could stop her. All were amazed at Grandma's "return to the world." I whispered to myself, "If I ever get out of here (that's how I felt), I'm going to do this work."

I promptly forgot this promise until some years later when my then husband suggested, "Do what you're good at!" And lo and behold, seven uphill years including 3,000 hours as an intern and passing State Board exams, I became a Licensed Marriage Family Therapist. I opened a small private practice the moment I turned fifty.

Lots of small, small things led to my return to life, including lots of hard work with my doctor and myself. I had to come to grips with my limits. I absolutely had to put my health first. I knew if I did not have my mental health my life would be worth nothing.

But back to my hospitalization. As a nun, I'd been called by God into a fine teaching community. I had taught in South Central Los Angeles (the "hood" then) and adored my kids and every inch of my service. I was called by God at an early age to help the poor and abandoned. I just never knew quite how that would work out.

On my first "pass" from the unit, I got to take a walk down Santa Monica Boulevard. It was an exquisite day of blue sky, light and sunny fresh air. Suddenly, I felt with my entire being this message:

> *I called you into this committed life and*
> *(after 20 years) I am now calling you out.*

God spoke to my being and in that moment I heard my permission to take a medical leave and re-examine my 36 years. I knew that moment that I could ask for a medical leave from the community and heal. I moved from the psych unit into my own furnished apartment in Santa Monica. I knew nothing of managing money, being single or of the world!

So, the end of my story? That dreadful nightmare took me by surprise in the summer of '72. I spent six long weeks in the hospital. Since that time, I met and married a wonderful man who helped me center and stabilize my life.

I earned two graduate degrees and have held responsible positions. I attempted these challenges when I felt better and felt I had regained my strength. I wanted to prove to myself that I was 100% A-OK.

Do I have occasional "bad" days? Yes, we all do. Am I afraid that "it" will ever happen again? Down deep in my heart I must have a healthy respect for my own limits. But most of the time this blessed nightmare is long past. This experience was a gift, a blessing in disguise that offered me the possibility to make a major change in my life and live a happy, fulfilling new Journey.

The Third Stranger

I had met my ever-faithful rock of a husband, Paul, at my age 37, his 27. He had not a moment of religious training but was a deeply spiritual young guy.

I was 37 going on 15 emotionally, sexually. I was embarrassingly immature. There was not a lot of talking, but a one-ness, a rhythm. I not only discovered I loved him, but really adored him. And he believed in me. We were a team. He chopped wood and I stacked and carried logs to the many fires that we loved. He planted roses (300 plus) and I pruned. We traveled easily all over the world. We didn't fight, hardly ever. We used to observe couples who were snarly on their vacations, at airports or at dinner. I said, "What a shame to fight on vacation. What a waste of time and money."

Paul was not so affectionate. He was nit-picky to a fault. He was not the usual gift giver. He refused to acknowledge Hallmark's Valentine's Day, but he had his own way of showing affection. One day I brought home tomatillos (we loved them). Later Paul said, "I planted tomatillos, they should be ripe by your birthday!" That was better than any valentine.

On May 10, 2014 Paul stayed with me 4 ½ hours to see me through surgery for non-smokers lung cancer. I should say this was my second cancer surgery. My first, for colon cancer, was in 2010. Later he told me he thought I'd died. Three days later, I left the hospital to come home to recover. One week later, I saw Paul standing in the kitchen, dressed for a trip, his packed suitcase on the floor. I pointed. He said, "I'm going to Hawaii." I asked, "Now?" No one deserved a trip more than Paul, but this was not how we rolled. He said, "I put it on the calendar last night." I said, "I didn't notice." Then he went to the garage, started the Lexus and pulled away.

I was stunned.

I later found out that he went to Hilo, a place we never traveled together. That trip was the severing, the beginning of our end, the end of our sweet, lovely accidental meeting in August 1973. Now he was 68 and I 78, verging on our Golden Years. No more till death do us part.

The beginning of our end. It was not my choice to sell our house, our former home, or file for divorce. Paul left for his new life and I discovered him on the senior dating site, "Our Time," where he described himself as widowed and searching for the same. The next Stranger

Within me appeared then to shock me out of my peace and stability.

The Fourth Stranger

As my health and marriage were falling apart, I knew I needed to write. In May of 2014, I began working one-on-one with Mary Tuchscherer, my writing teacher. She gently led me to unlock my self-consciousness and to face my humiliating fears.

Although I never intended those very private thoughts to turn into a book, Karen Mireau encouraged me to see the poetry in my story. The thought of publishing terrified me, but as I wrote, I gradually made peace with my past. I now stand alone in my truth and walk into each tomorrow with courage and gratitude.

In 2016, she (I) woke up as Maure, divorced, settled and sobbing within the grief I couldn't seem to flood out of the 80-year-old me, who'd survived several lifetimes, meeting the Stranger I am now, standing alone. I will always wonder who I was then with Paul. What did I, or what did we, miss? And what else do I have to realize, learn, deepen, and grow?

My Friendly Strangers

Every single minute I've lived brings me to this place of knowing me. Realizing who in the world I am now, who I will become, until the Strangers are all one and life transforms into the Eternal Now. No more mystery, no more sorrow. All is known.

Letter
to the
Stranger
Within

2

I become real
 like the Velveteen Rabbit
 life weary and a bit faded, but loved
 by God, saints, angels and even myself

I become real
 by staying attentive, open and clear
 standing firmly on my own two legs
 and accepting my history

I become real
 by pitching, sorting, choosing
 evolving, releasing people and things that do not
 serve me and getting my financial life straight

I become real
 as I turn 80
 and I become even realer, risking all
 standing naked in the town square

4

Naked in the town square
    I turn 80, an elder now
    mysterious, unexplained
    bleached by age, wizened by time

Naked in the town square
    a scraggly, spindly tree with lacy branches
    rising out of a solid trunk
    stretches against a darkening sky

Naked in the town square
    a storm arrives
    and there appears: a double rainbow
    my tree a silhouette behind

Naked in the town square
    my tree stands for hope, for what I might become
    for the strangeness of this long journey
    the gift of my most blessed life

Not by choice
> Am I transforming my life
> looking at hard truths
> with the eyes of a Stranger

Not by choice
> Am I almost 80, abandoned
> selling our home, now house
> and looking for a place to live, alone

Not by choice
> Am I accepting life's crushing blows
> yet choosing to explore, expand
> and live my life fully

Not by choice
> Am I now broken wide
> still made of flesh and blood
> and heart and soul

I will never forget
     how we met
     you were 27
     I was 37 going on 15

I will never forget
     saying: "I will never catch up to you financially."
     and you replied, with an immeasurable gift
     "You bring things that money can't buy."

I will never forget
     how you stood by me
     how you believed in me
     and seemed to truly love me

I will never forget
     how after 32 years you left me
     days after my lung cancer surgery
     only a mark on the calendar to let me know

In the beginning
> we walked along the Bay
> before the Big Bang of falling in love
> becoming steadfast, accidental friends

In the beginning
> we found a first home
> a place for our love to flourish
> then more homes in the East Bay

In the beginning
> later there were apples and apricots
> plums and palm trees—and roses
> 300 roses—planted just for me

In the beginning
> there were bevies of quail each spring
> fawns and does that came to bless us
> a white owl who-whooing in the tallest palm

In the beginning
> there were winter fires
> you cut wood, we stacked it
> and together we kept ourselves warm

At the end
>   you list yourself on a dating site
>   as "widowed," not divorced
>   you disappear to Hawaii
>   alone and unknown

At the end
>   we meet on a cold November morning
>   at "The Settlement Conference"
>   (as if loving someone for 32 years
>   could ever really be final)

At the end
>   twice you say, "I am sorry."
>   "I want to believe you," I whisper
>   you say, "You are the only one on earth
>   who ever really loved me." I say, "I know."

At the end
>   You say, "I always loved you, but
>   I cannot undo what is done."
>   the silent doors close, I walk out
>   into the damp air, my own perfect Stranger

14

The dark losses
     reveal themselves so slowly
     I couldn't absorb this amputation
     any other way

The dark losses
     amplified by having trusted
     so wholeheartedly and unconditionally
     only to be thrown away

The dark losses
     calling me to be re-Christened
     reborn at 80
     to move forward step-by-baby step

The dark losses
     leading to a path of knowing
     uncharted truths
     a new universe of hope

Now what?
>   where have my days gone
>   my time amorphous, slipping from me

Now what?
>   loose ends of my life
>   filled with incompleteness, uncertainty

Now what?
>   my past life a mirage
>   in the rear view mirror

Now what?
>   gradually healing, accepting, realizing
>   life as I've lived it is gone

When I received the habit in 1956
        the early nun
        I labored over sewing it endlessly

When I received the habit
        it was all a blur of black skirts and capes
        and granny shoes

When I received the habit
        my hair was chopped short, all vanity erased
        I sensed dignity, poise and self-containment
        or maybe not . . .

When I received the habit
        exhaustion, chronic migraines
        and the drain of my confidence
        told another, hidden story

I'm tired of being Good
      too Good for my own Good
      little Goody-Two-Shoes
      Good Good Good

I'm tired of being Good
      I know Good, do I ever!
      but was I really Good
      or just flying under the radar?

I'm tired of being Good
      of not upsetting the apple cart
      of avoiding flak
      staying out of the fray

I'm tired of being Good
      as much as I love God and Good-ness
      I'm tired of rules
      now all I want to be is free

The past
       is what fuels our future, eventually
       whether we like it or not

The past
       reminds us what a blessing it is that we don't know
       the tomorrows to come

The past
       is what we must shed, slip out of like an old skin
       to allow the journey to continue

The past
       is the source of new-born hope and energy
       and faith in our selves

Accept things as they are
      then allow them to mulch

Accept things as they are
      then let them transform in time

Accept things as they are
      then release betrayal

Accept things as they are
      and find the richness in my history

Something split open then
　　　for my 50th birthday I bought myself
　　　an amethyst geode, a stone-grey womb
　　　and I broke off pieces to give away

Something split open now
　　　ungodly shock and pain
　　　unreal plummeting into a nether world
　　　my old life a memory

Something split open
　　　maybe my precious heart
　　　perceptions of my reality
　　　my trust in my old life

Something split open
　　　an open heart surgery
　　　without anesthetic
　　　a fierce, earthquake severing

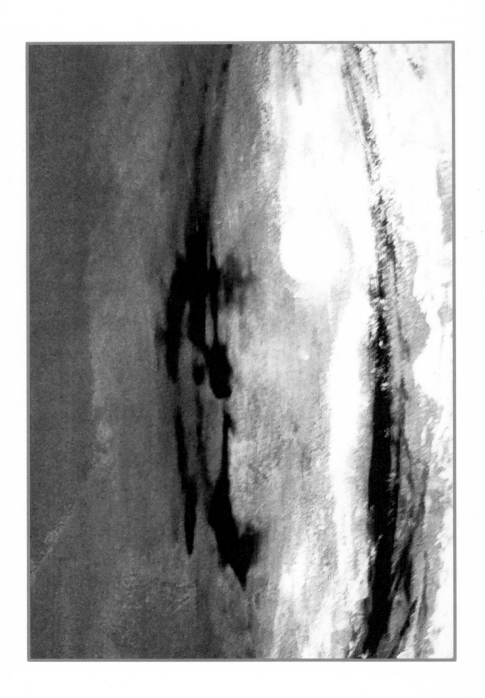

Be open
>   and wary

Be open
>   and protective

Be open
>   and take care

Be open
>   and move forward

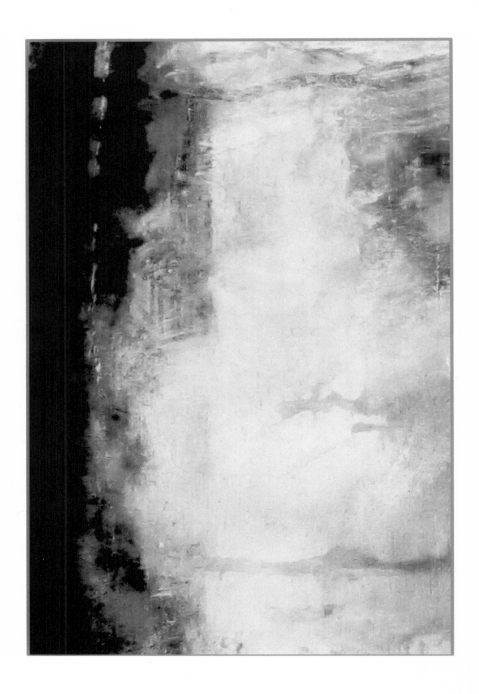

I imagined I'd grow into wisdom
>   when I observed the grace, knowing and calm
>   of grandmothers, long-time wives
>   and gracious single women, sister celibates

I imagined I'd grow into wisdom
>   when our Mother died unexpectedly at 54
>   and as the eldest of seven children
>   death became a natural part of my history

I imagined I'd grow into wisdom
>   when mentors Myra Barbeau and Charlotte Green
>   both mothers in their 40s and ahead of their time
>   left this Earth the same summer of 1974

I imagined I'd grow into wisdom
>   not knowing I'd be blessed with the privilege
>   of living to my 80s still with miles and miles to go
>   to become like those women I admire

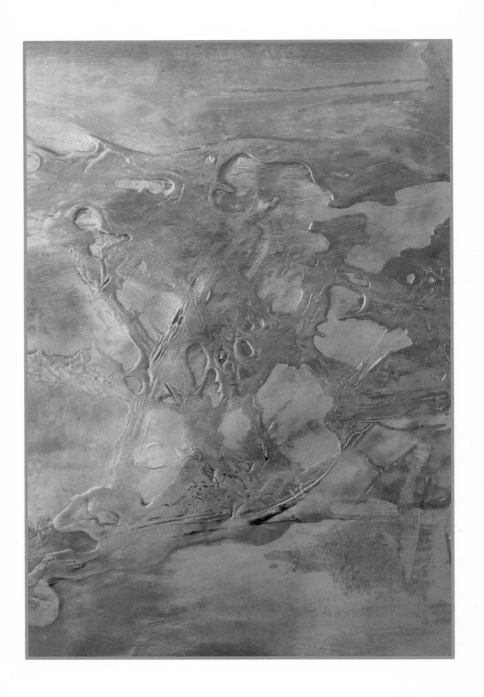

My Mother arrives in a dream
  to join me at the kitchen table
  brown eyes clear, steady, soft, loving
  her hair glorious white from age 34

My Mother arrives in a dream
  to offer a handmade, artful bag
  with the Book of Life inside
  encased in an exquisite red leather cover

My Mother arrives in a dream
  I want to know so many things . . . how is heaven?
  are you whole, complete, transformed, at peace?
  there is much to share, but we do not speak

My Mother arrives in a dream
  you left so early, so unexpectedly, so permanently
  I love you so . . . please come again and stay awhile
  please never leave me alone again

Splinters of memory
        like a shattered glass
        you never told me your story, Mother
        there was so much I never knew and never asked

Splinters of memory
        a Brooklyn-born girl
        you left high school to work as a secretary
        to give your three brothers an education

Splinters of memory
        you married a Navy man
        who gave you seven children
        then left you to die alone, so alone

Splinters of memory
        As a child, I kept heartaches and worries from you
        but now, at 80, I would give anything
        to know you, and to show you who I have become

What I know
> and don't know, after 80 years
> is massive, infinite, mysterious
> beyond understanding

What I know
> is to listen to my inner voices
> to the quiet guidance
> I've always heard in times of distress

What I know
> is that I am protected, informed, blessed
> by Angels, Saints and those friends
> who have gone before me

What I know
> is that I have never not believed
> and trusted
> in the kaleidoscope of surprise "aha" moments

Healing
>   of this magnitude
>   is lava slow
>   so slow it seems not to be

Healing
>   in tiny breaths
>   signs of new life and hope
>   oh so slowly

Healing
>   air, light, nurturing sky
>   green hills, ground me
>   gently guide me

Healing
>   a toothless orphan cat
>   with green loving eyes
>   comes to comfort me

Comfy, my soul cat
        with exquisite green eyes
        a milky white underbelly

Comfy, my soul cat
        once homeless street cat
        toothless, craving treats

Comfy, my soul cat
        purring in contralto
        my best anti-depressant

Comfy, my soul cat
        my nighttime protector
        my precious comfort

Truth echoes through me
    like a gentle wind
    the Maure I was then who gave of herself
    every thought, every ounce, every inch

Truth echoes through me
    how I volunteered my life to God
    for nearly 20 years, then left
    with a $200 plus interest dowry in my pocket

Truth echoes through me
    a novice: still evolving
    still ignorant of money
    without street smarts though I served in 'the hood'

Truth echoes through me
    like a gentle wind
    the Maure I am now
    still the same, yet so different

44

Aging, a new part of my journey
    long friendships, sacred history with clients
    new friends and Angels coming my way
    to love, support, encourage and teach me

Aging, a new part of my journey
    I walk carefully this slippery slope
    one begun when I was born
    careful not to fall

Aging, yes I faint and fall unexpectedly
    lose my DMV privileges for seven months
    trade all my shoes
    for stable, old lady ones

Aging, a new part of my journey
    a silent sort of being, only hinted at before
    but now I glance in a store window
    not recognizing the woman I saw, the woman I am

Aging, a new part of my journey
    I begin to see myself as others must
    I learn to be at peace, become friends
    with the Stranger I recognize as me

Tomorrow is another day
        and if not
        it won't matter at all

Tomorrow is another day
        with unexpected twists and turns
        both hurdles and humbling moments

Tomorrow is another day
        as I continue to go gently
        into my new dark and unknown life

Tomorrow is another day
        with new blessings, ideas
        and . . . possibilities

In Gratitude

When one writes her first book at age 80,
she may be forgiven her long but essential list
of those who grew and supported her.

Comfort (Comfy) Quilter
Soul Cat writing companion who is
unconditionally present

Sister M. Laurentia Digges, Ph.D., CSJ (RIP)
Author, college counselor, charismatic teacher
of literature and theology, who taught me to
truly see trees.

Edward Colbert, MD (RIP)
First healer and psychiatrist par excellence.

My parents, Mary Ann and Edward S. Quilter
(RIP) and my brother and sisters:
Kathy Quilter (RIP), Patrick (RIP), Sheila,
Judith, Deborah, Monica Mary (RIP).

Susannah Kennedy Poppenseiker
Dearest Friend and Family

Those who led me through the Death Valley of
divorce to the light and my new life:
Jerry Chang, J.D.
Dana M. Jackson, Legal Assistant
Cazeaux Nordstrum, LMFT

Next of kin and Devoted Soul Sisters:

Connie Kinney
>Spiritual Healer and Forever Friend.

Charlotte Wolter, LMFT
>Unconditionally Devoted Friend, Office Sharer, Comfy's Godmother.

Colleen Hendricks
>Scribe, Tech Tutor, Keeper of Secrets.

Wise women who loved and supported me my whole life, especially in their nineties:

Aunt Pat Murray (95 years)
Aunt Fran Donovan, Godmother (97 years)

Rebecca Rose and beloved daughter,
>Vikki (RIP) who lives her Spirit Life and shares it with me.

Melissa (Missy) Casas
>Quail Court Cat Whisperer and wise beyond her years, who gifts me with exquisite sensitivity and immeasurable generosity.

Monica Aimar Schiff
>A Healer of Soul and Skin. A gifted presence.

Judi Amos
>Amazing hair therapist. Most loyal of friends.

My Garden Group (30-plus years): Here and in Heaven and ever-faithful, inspiring, devoted, out-of-this-world, quirky, eccentric, extraordinary women, mothers, daughters, friends, healers, wives:

Mary Lowen, MD
Liz Matuk, RNP
Guyla Ponomareff, J.D.
Carol Gegner, LMFT
Kathy Jones, LMFT
Charlotte Wolter, LMFT
Connie Kinney, Spiritual Healer
Marjorie Minger, LMFT (RIP)
Sondra Altman, MD (RIP)

Open Door Members: My deepest, loveliest "ducklings" who allowed me to help create a Sacred Circle and who inspire me still:

Saundra Alassio
Betsy Campisi
Linda Chinn
Linda Farmer
Shannon Keenan Pedroni
Sheri Kurland
Karen Victoria Latunski
Theresa McCarthy
Barbara Bonds McDaniel
Madonna Treadway

Three Brother Priests who blessed me as I left the Convent:

> Reverend Xavier Colleoni
>> an Italian missionary in South Central Los Angeles who founded St. Martin de Porres Counseling Center for me and was the only religious visitor to my Santa Monica apartment.
>
> Al Garrotto (Retired Priest)
>> who sent his devoted Italian Mother to my apartment to support me. A gift.
>
> Reverend Wil Smith
>> who worked with me at St. Emydius Parish and was dedicated and devoted to my eighth-graders and to me. He sent me a $200 check and said, "No thanks are needed, pass it on when you can." This was a huge gift, his entire months' salary at that time.

Last, but not least:

> Nona Mock Wyman, of Ming Quong (Radiant Light) store, a Writer of three memoirs who inspires and encourages me always.

Barbara Bonds McDaniel

About the Artist

Barbara Bonds McDaniel began her artistic life as a young girl. She dabbled in collage and painting techniques while in high school, but her real interest lay in three-dimensional art and architecture. This led to a long and very rich creative path as a real estate developer, a roll-up-your-sleeves home remodeler and as a passionate interior designer.

In 1994, tragedy struck when her young adult son, Eric, died during a hiking expedition. Barbara's life then took a different turn. In 1995 she enrolled in Holy Names University and received a Masters Degree in Spirituality. Shortly thereafter, she attended a class in dream interpretation with Pt. Reyes painter Toni Littlejohn. She began formally studying with Ms. Littlejohn and very quickly discovered that she was not a realistic painter, but was drawn to abstract images and botanical materials such as salt, sand, spices, and ash—all elements that appear in Barbara's work.

The deep shamanistic quality of Barbara's colorful paintings is only hinted at in the black and white versions presented in the interior of this book. They are fragments of larger works intended to reflect the dream-like life reflections of the poems by author Maure Quilter.

Maure Quilter, Age 3

About the Author

Maure Quilter was born in 1936 into a Navy family and she became a caretaker of her six younger siblings at a very early age. After attending five high schools, she entered Mt. Saint Mary's College. The following year she was accepted by the Sisters of St. Joseph of Carondelet where she served for 17 years.

In 1972, Maure left the convent and moved to San Francisco where she married, earned an MA in Administration and later an MA in Psychology. In 1986, at age 50, she received her LMFT license and began a private practice in Lafayette, California.

Maure began yet a new chapter in her life when at age 78, she underwent surgery for lung cancer. When her husband of 32 years left her, she found a new path opening.

Now in her 80th year, she continues her work in Spiritual Discernment, as a writer and in serving the world.

Comments, responses and reviews
are welcome at:
maurequilter@yahoo.com

To order more copies of this book
please visit
www.lulu.com

For events or interviews with the author
please email
Azalea.Art.Press@gmail.com